100 PLANTS
for
QUICK-GROWING
Gardens

100 PLANTS
—for—
QUICK-GROWING
Gardens

General Editor: Mary Moody

CRESCENT BOOKS
NEW YORK • AVENEL

Contributing writers: Mary Moody, Stephanie Watson

Published by Lansdowne Publishing Pty Ltd
Level 5, 70 George Street, Sydney NSW 2000, Australia

This 1995 edition published by Crescent Books,
distributed by Random House Value Publishing, Inc.,
40 Engelhard Avenue, Avenel, New Jersey 07001

Random House
New York • Toronto • London • Sydney • Auckland

First published 1994

© Copyright: Lansdowne Publishing Pty Ltd 1994
© Copyright design : Lansdowne Publishing Pty Ltd 1994

Managing Director: Jane Curry
Publishing Manager: Deborah Nixon
Production Manager: Sally Stokes
Project Coordinators/Editors: Kate Oliver and Bronwyn Hilton
Copy Editor: Doug Cooper
Horticultural Advisor: Liz Ball
Design Concept: Catherine Martin
Typesetter: Veronica Hilton
Formatted in Galliard on Quark Xpress
Printed in Singapore by Kyodo Printing Co (S'pore) Pte Ltd

ISBN 0-517-12134-4

A CIP catalog record for this book is available from the Library of Congress.

KEY TO SYMBOLS

○	prefers full sun
◑	prefers partial shade
●	prefers shade
pH̬	acid soil
p̂H	alkaline soil
❖	half-hardy – temperatures down to 0°C°
❖❖	hardy – temperatures down to -5°C
❖❖❖	fully hardy – temperatures down to -15°C

Contents

Introduction

Most gardeners are impatient, and dream of 'instant' results from their prized plants. However, many of the species that form the backbone of the garden, such as conifers, evergreen trees and shrubs, are slow growing, often taking decades to create the desired effect.

Fortunately, in nature there are a great many quick-growing plants which can be used to give fast results while the slower-growing species are getting established. Quick-growing plants can be used in many ways: as 'nursery' plants to protect smaller and more sensitive species until they are strong enough to survive the prevailing conditions; as background plants in a flowerbed or border; as hedges to provide privacy and shelter from prevailing winds; and as splashes of colour when the garden is looking bare or drab.

✿ **CAREFUL CULTIVATION** Whatever the reason for selecting these particular plants, care in their cultivation will always be vital to their success. Often, quick-growing plants are quite heavy feeders, quickly depleting the soil of both moisture and nutrients. For this reason, it is essential to build the soil up with plenty of organic matter in the form of well-rotted compost or manure prior to planting. Plants that have been well grown and provided with the correct growing conditions will not only perform at their best, they will also be resistant to disease and pest infestation.

Therefore, select plants that are suited to your particular climate, avoiding those that are frost sensitive if you live in an area that experiences heavy winter frosts, or heat sensitive if you live near the tropics. Inevitably, plants that are subjected to climates that are not similar to their native environment will always struggle, and frequently become subject to diseases or attack by insect pests.

✿ **HEALTHY SOIL** The soil is another important factor in maintaining the health of plants. Certain species have particular requirements for soil pH balance, either on the acid or alkaline side of the scale. Where this preference is important to their cultivation, it has been indicated alongside the name of the plant in the listing. If plants thrive in an alkaline soil, incorporate some dolomite lime at the rate indicated on the package to create the correct pH. If plants are acid loving, such as rhododendrons and azaleas, they should be fed with a specially formulated fertilizer to increase soil acidity, or the soil should be treated with powdered sulfur, which is slow acting but very effective.

Also take into account the texture of the soil in your garden. A majority of plants prefer soil that has good drainage, and this should always be established when you start to garden on a particular piece of land. Heavy, clay soils are sometimes slow to allow moisture to drain away, and this creates waterlogged conditions which are resented by the root systems of many species. Clay soils will need to be corrected with large quantities of compost or well-rotted manure, to provide aeration and improve drainage. In certain clay soils, the addition of gypsum will also help to correct poor drainage. In extreme situations, however, underground drainage pipes may need to be laid to take away excessive moisture from plant roots after heavy rain or routine watering.

Light, sandy soils can also be a problem. While they are very free-draining, they dry out very quickly after watering, and are usually low on essential nutrients. Again, the addition of quantities of organic matter will help to correct the soil texture, allowing it to hold moisture for longer periods.

✿ **THE MAGIC OF MULCH** The healthiest gardens are always well mulched, with a good layer of mulch surrounding plants from the time they are first positioned in the garden. A well-mulched garden requires less watering in summer, and the soil temperature is more evenly maintained. When organic mulches are used, plants will also be supplied with a steady quantity of nutrients, reducing the necessity for regular additional feeding. The best mulches are well-rotted manures and homemade compost, although straw, grass clippings, bark and leaf mulch are also frequently used. Ideally, a mixture of all these mulches will give the best results, with a sprinkling of blood and bone thrown in for good measure. This helps the mulch to break down, and adds to the feeding benefits. Begin by layering manure at ground level, then top this with a mixture of straw and leaves or grass clippings and leaves. As the mulch layers break down they can be replenished, to ensure continuous protection from weeds.

Some species dislike being mulched around the base of their stem or trunk, so avoid piling organic matter above ground level. In the case of young annual seedlings, thick mulch at the base will create very humid conditions, which can cause the stems to rot. Avoid this by leaving a gap between the base of the plant and the mulch, to allow the air to circulate freely around the plant.

✿ **PEST PREVENTION** By making sure that plants have the best possible growing conditions, you will also be helping them to withstand problems with pests and diseases. Select a planting position that matches their particular requirements for sun and shade, as once again they will be struggling to cope if placed in the shade when they need full sun. At best, they will fail to flower; at worst, they will become diseased and die. When shopping for plants from a nursery or plant store, always look for robust, disease-free specimens that appear to be growing in a good-quality potting mixture. Plants that have suffered from poor care while in their containers will seldom do well after transplanting into the garden. When you get the plants home, keep them in a sheltered, shaded corner and water them daily—twice daily if the weather is particularly hot or the potting soil appears to be drying out. Ideally, they should be planted out as quickly as possible, into well-prepared ground that has been watered thoroughly on the day before planting. Some species will require staking at the time of planting, to prevent them from being damaged by strong winds. Others may need protection from frost during their first year of growth, and this can be provided by partially covering them with shade cloth during winter.

Quick-growing trees: These can be used in many ways. If the garden is very open or exposed, trees can be used to form a hedge or windbreak, for both protection and privacy. Large growers with a spreading habit can be used as shade trees, while those with a particularly striking outline are generally used as feature or accent plants. Trees with slender, upright trunks can be group planted to form a copse, under which a variety of woodland plants can be added. Deciduous trees can be planted close to the house to provide shade in summer, while allowing the warmth of the winter sun to shine through. Always check the mature height and spread of a tree before buying it, to ensure that your garden is large enough to accommodate its growth.

Quick-growing shrubs: These will give substance and texture to the garden while the slower-growing species are getting established. Shrubs can be used as low hedges, or as bulk at the back of a flowerbed or border. They will provide a framework for other plantings, and their flowers will bring instant colour to the garden. Some shrubs eventually reach quite a large size, so again, make sure that they have sufficient room to grow comfortably to maturity.

Quick-growing climbers: These are vital for covering arches and pergolas, or for screening unattractive areas, such as a fence or shed. Fast climbers will soften architectural features and quickly provide a background for other plantings.

Quick-growing perennials: These will also give good results from the first year of planting, although most will continue to increase in size over a period of years. Many perennials die back in winter, bursting forth in spring with dramatic foliage followed by flowers. They can be planted in mixed beds or herbaceous borders, as accent plants, for colour and texture around a garden pool or waterfall, or a woodland setting. Most species listed are quite easy to grow, and will be very rewarding for years to come.

Quick-growing bulbs: These are wonderful 'fill-ins' for gaps and spaces in the garden, including flowerbeds, around shrubs, and beneath trees. They can be planted in clumps or drifts, or naturalized into the lawn for a woodland effect. Most bulbs can be left in the ground for many years, where they will multiply.

Quick-growing ground covers: Plants that cover the soil surface are very valuable because they act as a form of living mulch by supressing weed growth and helping to keep the soil moist. In new gardens it is important to establish some fast growing covers that will not only tie the landscape together visually, but help to reduce maintainence such as watering and weeding.

Quick-growing annuals: These are quite work intensive, as they will need to be sown or planted out as seedlings every year, with the exception of those species that self-sow and multiply in the garden without assistance. Annuals provide fast colour, and can also be grown effectively in containers.

✿ HOW TO USE THIS BOOK

This book has been designed as a simple guide to successfully cultivating all the plants listed. The soil pH level has been specified only when it needs to be either acid or alkaline, according to the particular requirements of the plant. All other plants can be easily grown in soil in the neutral range (that is, pH 7.0). Refer to the key to symbols on page 4.

A plant's preference for sun, partial shade or full shade, and its hardiness rating are also indicated by symbols. The hardiness symbols indicate each individual plant's ability to withstand winter temperatures and frost. No symbols have been given for annuals, which are only grown from spring to autumn in cool and cold climates, and therefore are not expected to survive winter.

The mature height of plants, indicated under 'Description', may vary from one climate to another, sometimes only reaching the maximum size in the country in which it is a native species.

Where advice has been given on pests and disease infestations, this is meant as a guide to a certain plant's susceptibility to a particular problem. Treatment of that problem will vary from one country to another.

Albizia julibrissin
Silk tree ○ ◐ p̂H ❖❖

✿ **DESCRIPTION** A popular, deciduous tree that doesn't grow too large, reaching a height of 25 feet (7.5 m) with an equal spread when mature. The silk tree may have single or multiple trunks and produces attractive horizontal branches, bearing soft fern-like leaves that fold up at night. Its pink flowers are grouped and have a fluffy appearance, and are followed by clusters of long, brown seed pods during autumn. The silk tree is hardy to wind, pollution, drought, and frost, but is short-lived relative to other trees. ✿ **PLANTING** The silk tree will tolerate most soils, however sandy and well-drained types are best. A sunny position will encourage prolific flowering, but light shade is tolerated. Plant during spring.
✿ **FLOWERING** Once established, the tree will flower from late spring to summer. ✿ **CULTIVATION** Keep moist throughout summer, but avoid overwatering. Fertilizing is not essential, but an application of pulverized manure during spring will boost new growth. During winter or early spring, lightly prune to maintain the tree's natural shape. During winter in the coldest of districts, it is advisable to wrap the trunks with hessian while they are establishing. Remove the tree completely when it begins to lose its vigour. ✿ **PROPAGATION** By seed in autumn.

Betula pendula
Silver birch ○ ❖❖❖

✿ **OTHER NAMES** Birch, European white birch

✿ **DESCRIPTION** A highly ornamental, deciduous tree with smooth, silvery bark and slender arching branches. The silver birch usually grows to a height of 30 feet (9 m) with a spread of 10–15 feet (3–4.5 m). The leaves are diamond-shaped turning gold during autumn, and the vibrant bark is decoratively marked. The flowers are insignificant but are followed by yellowish, pendulous catkins. As they ripen and disintegrate, a mass of winged seeds are released. ✿ **PLANTING** Silver birches are best grown as specimen trees or planted during winter alongside dark green evergreens in a sunny, open position. They tolerate poorer soils but must have good drainage. Stake the trees when young. ✿ **FLOWERING** Catkins appear in summer.

✿ **CULTIVATION** Silver birches are relatively pest free and require very little maintenance. An annual feed during spring will induce plenty of lush new growth, and regular watering during the hot summer months will prevent the tree's roots from wandering too far. Silver birch roots have been known to enter drainpipes, so if possible keep them well away. Mulch around the tree to preserve soil moisture and prune only if necessary during late autumn to prevent excessive bleeding. ✿ **PROPAGATION** Collect the seed during autumn and sow in sterilized seed-raising mix the following spring.

Cornus florida

Flowering dogwood ○ ◑ ❖❖❖

✿ **OTHER NAMES** Eastern flowering dogwood, Common dogwood, American boxwood ✿ **DESCRIPTION** A charming, spreading deciduous tree that is considered one of the finest trees native to Northern America. Growing to 40 feet (8 m) in height, the dogwood has a pleasant shape and masses of oval, deep green leaves that change to a magnificent reddish-purple in autumn. It is the spring display, however, for which the plant is most admired. The flowers are insignificant, but the showy, pinkish-white bracts make a wonderful sight when the tree is covered with them in late spring. ✿ **PLANTING** Bare-rooted trees can be planted in winter, or potted varieties in spring or autumn. Choose well-drained soil that is moderately rich and moisture retentive. Use stakes to support the young tree for the first few years if planted in a windy or exposed situation. ✿ **FLOWERING** Flower bracts appear in late spring. ✿ **CULTIVATION** Mulch around the base of the tree to prevent the soil from drying out in summer, but take care not to bring the mulch too close to the trunk, as it may cause fungal problems. Water well during hot, dry weather to encourage deep root growth. ✿ **PROPAGATION** From seed sown in autumn, or softwood cuttings taken in summer.

Elaeagnus angustifolia
Oleaster ○ ❖❖❖

❀ **OTHER NAME** Russian olive ❀ **DESCRIPTION** The oleaster is a small, deciduous tree that grows to a height of 10–15 feet (3–4 m), with an equal spread. Valued for its attractive silver-grey foliage, and its ability to withstand strong winds and city smog, the oleaster makes a useful windbreak plant. When mature, the trunk becomes gnarled and crooked, and the bark develops a shredded appearance. During early summer, tiny, bell-shaped, fragrant flowers emerge, followed by small, oval-shaped, edible yellow fruits that the birds relish. ❀ **PLANTING** For best results, choose an open, sunny position with well-drained soil. The oleaster is not fussy about pH and minimal soil preparation is required. Plant during winter or early spring. ❀ **FLOWERING** Flowers emerge during early summer. ❀ **CULTIVATION** The oleaster is virtually pest free and will withstand drought and frost. Prune during winter or early spring to remove any unwanted growth. Occasionally, the small, central branches may die when they can no longer compete with the outer branches for light. These can be pruned away at any time of year and will reveal the unusual trunk. Feed during spring with a light dressing of complete fertilizer to encourage flowering and the formation of fruits. ❀ **PROPAGATION** By seed in autumn or semi-hardwood cuttings in summer.

Ficus carica

Fig ○ p̂H ❖❖❖

❀ **DESCRIPTION** A beautiful, fast-growing deciduous tree that bears
delicious brown, green, or purple, pear-shaped fruit when ripe. The
common fig will grow to a height of 20 feet (6 m) with a spread at least
equal to its height, and the large, dark green leaves provide a notable
contrast to the smooth, grey bark. Minute flowers form inside the fruit.
Most figs will bear fruit after a period of four years and produce one or two
crops per year. ❀ **PLANTING** For best results, plant during midwinter or
early spring into rich, moist soil in a sunny, protected position.

❀ **FLOWERING** Minute flowers form inside the fruit and fruiting may
occur during early spring or summer, depending upon the variety.

❀ **CULTIVATION** Too much fertilizer will produce rapid growth at the
expense of the fruit. A moderate dressing of complete fertilizer during
spring is all that is required. Overwatering should also be avoided, as it may
cause the figs to split. Prune long branches back quite hard during winter
and remove any crossing branches or suckers. As the fruit ripens, watch out
for the birds. ❀ **PROPAGATION** The lower branches are easily layered
during summer; suckers can be divided; or dormant cuttings can be taken
during winter.

Fraxinus excelsior

Common ash ○ ◑ ❖❖❖

❀ **OTHER NAMES** European ash, English ash ❀ **DESCRIPTION**
This tree has the ability to thrive in a variety of climates and soils. It is
deciduous and grows to a height of 20–30 feet (6–9 m) with a spread of
20 feet (6 m), making it a popular choice for large parks and gardens. Ashes
have decorative, pinnate leaves and today there are many interesting cultivars
available. The flowers are greenish-white or brownish-purple, tiny in size, and
appear in dense clusters. They are soon followed by new foliage growth and a
mass of narrow, winged seeds, which cling to the tree until autumn or early
winter. ❀ **PLANTING** Take care when positioning an ash as the large,
surface-feeding roots could undermine foundations and drainage systems,
particularly if water is in short supply. Plant in early spring into moist, deep,
and well-drained soil. They will tolerate a windy position in full sun or part
shade and are resistant to pollution. ❀ **FLOWERING** Flowers appear
during spring. ❀ **CULTIVATION** Water deeply throughout summer and
feed during spring to satisfy the hungry, searching roots. Young trees may be
lightly pruned during autumn; however, mature European ashes rarely
require pruning. ❀ **PROPAGATION** By seed in spring.

Jacaranda mimosifolia
Jacaranda ○ ❖

✿ **OTHER NAMES** Rosewood, Beautiful Brazilian tree

✿ **DESCRIPTION** The jacaranda is a most captivating and memorable spring-flowering, deciduous tree. It grows to a height of 30 feet (10 m) with a spread of 15 feet (5 m) and is able to thrive in a variety of climates. The jacaranda is furnished with attractive, pale-green, fern-like leaves and during spring, the bare branches produce stunning panicles of lavender-blue flowers. The display, notably better during a dry year, looks particularly effective when the jacaranda is grown near other spring-flowering trees with red blooms, such as *Brachychiton acerifolius* (Flame tree). Frost tender, it can also be grown as a potted specimen in a greenhouse. ✿ **PLANTING** Plant during late winter or early spring in a sunny and protected position. Jacarandas are not particularly fussy about the type of soil they grow in, so long as it is reasonably well drained. ✿ **FLOWERING** Flowering usually occurs during late spring, but the flowering time may be delayed by several weeks in cooler areas. ✿ **CULTIVATION** Jacarandas seem to thrive on neglect. Keep them on the dry side during late winter and early spring but water regularly after the flowers have fallen. Feed during summer to maintain vigour. Prune young jacarandas after flowering, to prevent them from developing an ungainly appearance. ✿ **PROPAGATION** Collect the ripened seed in late autumn and sow the following spring.

Juglans regia
Walnut ○ ❖❖❖

❀ **OTHER NAME** English walnut, Persian walnut

❀ **DESCRIPTION** The walnut is a stately, deciduous, shade tree valued for its timber and tasty, edible nuts. Within 20 years, it may reach a height of 25 feet (7.5 m) or more, but will eventually grow much taller. The foliage is aromatic, bronze-purple in colour when young, turning glossy and green at maturity. Springtime sees the inconspicuous, green blossoms emerge in tandem with the new leaves. During summer, clusters of catkins appear, followed by the hard-coated nuts. ❀ **PLANTING** English walnuts require a deep, well-drained, fertile soil to accommodate their large, spreading roots, in an open, sunny position. Plant bare-rooted trees during midwinter, allowing ample room, as the roots secrete a substance known as juglone that inhibits the growth of nearby trees. ❀ **FLOWERING** Flowers appear during spring, followed by a mass of catkins and, eventually, the nuts.

❀ **CULTIVATION** Water deeply all summer, and feed with complete fertilizer and generous quantities of organic matter during spring. Mulching is also beneficial. To prevent excessive bleeding, prune to shape during summer or autumn. It may take up to 10 years for the nuts to form, depending upon the variety. Fallen nuts should be collected promptly and dried in the sun.

❀ **PROPAGATION** By seed in autumn.

Laburnum anagyroides
Common laburnum ○ ◐ ṗH ❖❖❖

✿ **OTHER NAME** Golden chain ✿ **DESCRIPTION** During late spring, the bright-yellow blooms of the common laburnum create a real showpiece in the garden. The large, pea-type flowers hang en masse, in attractive, pendulous clusters. These are followed by green, pea-shaped seed pods in autumn, which later turn brown. The leaves are dull green and downy in appearance and also hang gracefully from the tree. The common laburnum is deciduous and spreading in nature, may have single or multiple trunks, and reaches a height of about 20 feet (6 m) at maturity. All parts of the plant are poisonous to eat, particularly the seeds. ✿ **PLANTING** Plant during winter or early spring into deep, moist, and well-drained soil that is slightly alkaline in pH. Choose a position that receives full sun or light shade and protection from strong winds. Tall specimens should be staked until they are well established. In areas where rabbits reside, surround the tree with wire mesh for protection. ✿ **FLOWERING** Flowers appear during mid-spring in the first year. ✿ **CULTIVATION** Water generously throughout summer, and feed in early spring with pulverized manure. After flowering, prune to encourage bushiness, removing weakened or damaged branches. The green seed pods should also be removed if young children play nearby. ✿ **PROPAGATION** By seed or budding.

Liquidambar styraciflua

Liquidambar ○ ◑ ❖❖❖

✿ **OTHER NAME** American sweet gum ✿ **DESCRIPTION** Liquid-amber is one of the most highly prized trees for autumn foliage displays. It is a pyramidal-shaped, deciduous tree capable of growing up to 73 feet (22 m) high in cultivation, with the longer, lower branches spreading out to 45 feet (15 m). Throughout summer, the liquidambar is clothed in attractive, bright green, palmate leaves and when autumn arrives, they are transformed into a kaleidoscope of colour ranging from the deepest scarlet through to gold. During spring, they develop clusters of small, green flowers that are prickly in appearance. ✿ **PLANTING** These handsome trees require plenty of room to grow and are best planted away from drains and foundations. Plant during winter into deep, moist soil in a sunny or partially shaded position.
✿ **FLOWERING** Flowers appear from spring through to summer.
✿ **CULTIVATION** To prevent the liquidambar's extensive root system from wandering too far, be judicious with its food and water requirements. Feed with a slow-release, organic fertilizer in spring and autumn and keep the tree well watered. Prune during winter if necessary. ✿ **PROPAGATION** The seed should be collected during autumn, stratified and sown straight away, although the resultant seedlings will vary considerably in their autumn tones. Root cuttings can also be taken.

Malus floribunda
Japanese crab ○ ◐ ❖❖❖

❧ **OTHER NAMES** Japanese flowering crab apple

❧ **DESCRIPTION** An ideal tree for the home garden, the crab apple is prized for its abundant, sweetly-scented blossoms. A deciduous tree with arching branches that flower during spring it grows to a height of 25 feet (8 m) with a spread of 10 feet (3 m). The rose-coloured buds open into soft pink blooms and later fade to white. After flowering, the summer foliage bursts forth and is later enhanced by small cherry-like fruits that cling to the tree until late autumn. ❧ **PLANTING** Plant in winter into rich, moist, and well-drained soil. They flower most profusely in an open, sunny position but will also tolerate light shade. Grow away from paths and driveways, where the fruits can make a slippery mess. ❧ **FLOWERING** Blossoms appear from early spring through to early summer. ❧ **CULTIVATION** Crab apples can withstand frost but do not like dry soils. Water liberally in spring and summer, and feed in spring to aid the formation of flowers and fruits. Regular pruning is not required, other than a light trim after flowering during the tree's formative years. ❧ **PROPAGATION** By budding or grafting onto a suitable rootstock.

Populus nigra 'Italica'
Lombardy poplar ○ ❖❖❖

✿ **OTHER NAMES** Italian poplar, Pyramidal poplar
✿ **DESCRIPTION** A very fast-growing, spreading deciduous tree that is valued for its striking foliage, which changes shade according to the season. Growing to 90 feet (30 m) in the right situation, this tree has attractive, dark brown bark and diamond-shaped leaves which are bronze in spring, turning to brilliant green in summer, then to a rich yellow in autumn. ✿ **PLANTING** Choose a sunny, open position and deep, well-drained soil that has been enriched with plenty of organic matter prior to planting. Stake young trees to protect them from strong winds during the first few years' growth. Poplars cannot tolerate dry soil, and should be planted away from houses, as their roots can undermine foundations. ✿ **FLOWERING** Male trees produce red catkins in mid-spring. ✿ **CULTIVATION** Water well during summer, and mulch the soil surface to prevent the soil from drying out. Poplars will throw suckers, which can be a nuisance if they take root in the lawn or garden beds. Often poplars are planted as a fast-growing screen, then removed when other, less invasive plants have become established. ✿ **PROPAGATION** By hardwood cuttings taken in winter.

Prunus cerasifera

Cherry plum ○ pH ❖❖❖

✿ **OTHER NAME** Myrobalan ✿ **DESCRIPTION** A delightful,
spring blossom tree that grows up to 20–25 feet (6–7.5 m) with an equal
spread. The cherry plum is a bushy, round-headed tree that produces dense
masses of white, rose-like blossoms. Mature trees produce edible yellow or
red cherry-plums after flowering. Other attractive cultivars have been
derived from the cherry plum, such as *Prunus* 'Pissardii', which has beautiful
purple foliage and pale pink buds. *Prunus* 'Nigra' has dark purple foliage,
and as the name implies, appears almost black. ✿ **PLANTING** Plant bare-
rooted trees during late winter in light to medium, well-drained soil. Cherry
plums require an open, sunny position in order to flower well.
✿ **FLOWERING** Blossoms appear during spring. ✿ **CULTIVATION**
Cherry plums have shallow roots, so keep them well watered and mulched
throughout the summer months. During spring, an application of compost
and manure will encourage new growth. They can withstand hard pruning
if necessary, and this should be carried out during early winter. Otherwise,
prune only to maintain the bushy appearance. ✿ **PROPAGATION**
Cherry plums are mostly worked onto stocks of *Prunus myrobalana* and
Prunus marianna.

Robinia pseudoacacia

False acacia ○ ◐ ❖❖❖

✿ **OTHER NAME** Black locust ✿ **DESCRIPTION** Robinias will thrive almost anywhere, even in the poorest of soils, and will reward you every year. They are also particularly hardy in coastal areas and are widely grown through-out Europe and North America. Robinias are a deciduous tree that can reach a height of 30 feet (9 m) with a 6 feet (2 m) spread after 20 years. If permitted, they will eventually grow much taller. Pale green, fern-like leaves cast dappled shadows in the sun and the gnarled trunk and branches develop character with age. The autumn leaves turn yellow and luxurious panicles of scented, creamy-white flowers appear early in spring, which are promptly followed by a cascade of reddish-brown seed pods. ✿ **PLANTING** Choose a spacious, preferably sunny position with well-drained soil. Planting is best carried out during late winter or early spring when the soil is moist.
✿ **FLOWERING** Flowering occurs throughout spring, over a period of a month. ✿ **CULTIVATION** Keep the tree well watered throughout summer and fertilize during spring. Pruning is best carried out during late summer or early autumn to prevent unnecessary bleeding. Remember to remove any emerging suckers also. ✿ **PROPAGATION** Sow seeds in early spring, or divide the suckers leaving a piece of root attached.

Salix babylonica
Weeping willow ○ ◑ ❖❖❖

✿ **OTHER NAME** Babylon weeping willow ✿ **DESCRIPTION** When you think of weeping willows, visions of river banks shrouded in graceful, hanging branches may come to mind and rightfully so, as willows are great lovers of water. The weeping willow grows worldwide and is often seen gracing the gardens of large estates. It is a deciduous tree and is capable of reaching 50 feet (15 m) in height with an equal spread. Its weeping branches almost touch the ground and blow gently in the breeze. It has narrow, lime-green leaves that turn yellow during autumn. Pale yellowish-green catkins appear during spring. ✿ **PLANTING** Plant from autumn to spring in a sunny or partially shaded position. Ideally, the soil should be deep, moist, fertile, and well drained; they can withstand damp conditions. Give regular, deep waterings while they are establishing, and allow ample room to grow. Never be tempted to plant a weeping willow near a drain or house foundation, because the root system is extremely invasive and destructive. ✿ **FLOWERING** Inconspicuous catkins form during spring. ✿ **CULTIVATION** Trim the lower branches during winter and remove any dead branches. Keep the tree particularly moist during warm weather and feed in spring with a general purpose fertilizer. During summer, watch for any indication of rust. ✿ **PROPAGATION** By semi-ripe cuttings in summer and hardwood cuttings in winter.

Tamarix parviflora

Tamarisk ○ ❖❖❖

✿ **OTHER NAME** Early tamarisk ✿ **DESCRIPTION** The Tamarix genus is valued for its resistance to exposure and strong winds, making the trees ideal for hedges and screens trees in coastal or country gardens that have little protection. *Tamarix parviflora* is a small deciduous tree, growing to 15 feet (4 m) in height, with elegant stems covered in reddish bark and tiny, scale-like leaves. In spring, the last season's stem growth is covered with very small, pale pink, heath-like flowers that make a soft and pretty display. ✿ **PLANTING** This adaptable plant can be grown in quite poor soils, providing the drainage is good. It can also withstand dry summers, which makes it ideal for areas with a low rainfall. Choose a sunny, open position, and mulch around the base of the tree after planting.

✿ **FLOWERING** The flowers appear in profusion in early spring.

✿ **CULTIVATION** Pruning is essential to maintain a dense shape, encourage flowering, and prevent the plant from becoming straggly. Prune back hard after flowering, and the new growth will provide the flowering stems for the following spring. ✿ **PROPAGATION** By semi-ripe cuttings taken in spring, or hardwood cuttings taken in winter.

Buddleia davidii
Butterfly bush ○ ❖❖❖

❀ **OTHER NAME** Summer lilac ❀ **DESCRIPTION** No scented
garden would be complete without the hardy butterfly bush. The original
species produces lilac flowers with an orange centre. New cultivars, however,
produce a variety of colours, including white, dark purple, lilac, and purple-
red, and butterflies find them irresistible. *Buddleia davidii* is deciduous and
usually grows to a height of 7–9 feet (about 2–3 m), spreading to 6–8 feet
(1.5–2.5 m) at maturity. The branches are arching; the leaves are dark green,
lance-shaped, and velvety underneath. ❀ **PLANTING** Buddleias enjoy a
fertile, well-drained soil, but they can adapt to poorer soils. Choose a position
in full sun and plant at any time of year. In the coldest of regions, resist
planting until early spring. The butterfly bush is best situated in a mixed
shrub border or nearby a window so that its heavenly scent and little, winged
admirers can be fully appreciated. ❀ **FLOWERING** The long flower
spikes appear during summer and last through to late autumn or until the
first frost. ❀ **CULTIVATION** Apply a light dressing of complete fertilizer
during spring and keep them moist throughout summer. Flowers develop
on the current season's growth, so prune back hard during late winter.
❀ **PROPAGATION** Take softwood cuttings during late spring or early
summer, or semi-hardwood cuttings in late summer.

Colutea arborescens
Bladder senna ○ ❖❖❖

✿ **DESCRIPTION** A vigorous, rather coarse shrub, growing to 9 feet (3 m) in height, with a spreading, open habit. The foliage is small and pale green. The pea-like flowers are also quite small and appear in clusters. They are bright yellow, sometimes with a reddish tinge, blooming over several weeks in summer. The flowers are followed by bladder-like, reddish seed pods.

✿ **PLANTING** The value of this plant is its ease of cultivation, growing quickly in a wide range of soils and climates. Choose a sunny, open position, and virtually any garden soil that is not waterlogged. ✿ **FLOWERING** Flowers appear in summer. ✿ **CULTIVATION** This plant is very durable, and requires little or no attention once established. Water deeply during long, hot spells in summer, but take care not to overwater. Keep weeds from around the base of the plant, and mulch with leaves or bark to prevent new weed growth. Bladder senna can become a pest in the garden, as it self-seeds readily and new plants appear each spring. Remove them quickly before they have time to become established. ✿ **PROPAGATION** By softwood cuttings taken in summer, or from seed sown in autumn.

Cotinus coggygria
Smoke bush ○ ◑ ❖❖❖

❀ **OTHER NAMES** Smokewood, Smoke tree ❀ **DESCRIPTION** A handsome deciduous shrub that is prized for its foliage, flower heads, and autumn colourings. Smoke bush is a bushy plant that can grow and spread to 15 feet (5 m) if grown in the right situation. The leaves are oval or rounded, and a light green colour that turns yellow or red in autumn. The individual flowers are insignificant, however the entire flowerhead does give an impressive display, forming grayish, plume-like clusters that give the plant its common name. There are several interesting varieties, including 'Atropurpureus', which has reddish-purple foliage and flowers. ❀ **PLANTING** Although these plants give their best colours when situated in full sun, they can also be successfully grown in a semi-shaded situation. The soil should be well drained and fertile, but not over-rich, so avoid the addition of too much organic matter prior to planting. Plant in spring or summer, and water well until the shrub becomes well established. ❀ **FLOWERING** The flower heads should bloom from late summer onwards. ❀ **CULTIVATION** Mulch around the plant with leaf litter or well-rotted compost to suppress weeds and to prevent the soil from drying out. ❀ **PROPAGATION** Softwood cuttings can be taken in summer.

Fuchsia hybrids
Fuchsia ◑ ❖

✿ **DESCRIPTION** This large group of plants contains some really delightful flowering varieties that are easy to cultivate in a wide range of soils and climate conditions. They are deciduous or semi-evergreen in habit, losing their foliage only in colder climates when under stress. They can withstand temperatures down to 26°F (−5°C), however, they resent very long, hot summer temperatures. Fuchsias make excellent plants for containers, which makes them suitable for very cold or very hot climates, where they can be moved to shelter when necessary. The flowers and foliage vary considerably according to the variety, but all the flowers are tubular and pendulous, often with more than one petal colour. ✿ **PLANTING** Plant in a sheltered, semi-shaded situation in fertile soil that can be kept moist but still has excellent drainage. ✿ **FLOWERING** The flowering period is extensive, from early summer through to late autumn.
✿ **CULTIVATION** Mulch well with organic matter to provide slow-release nutrients, and to keep weed growth down. Water well, especially in summer, and stake those varieties where the weight of the flowers drags the stems onto the ground. ✿ **PROPAGATION** Very easily propagated with softwood cuttings taken at any time of the year.

Hydrangea macrophylla cultivars
Hydrangea ○ ◑ ❖❖❖

❀ **DESCRIPTION** A familiar, deciduous shrub with large pink, red, blue, or white blooms that usually grows to a height of 5–6 feet (1.5–2 m) and spreads 6–8 feet (2–2.5 m). The flower colour varies according to the pH of the soil, with the exception of the white varieties. Neutral or alkaline soils produce pink or red hydrangea blooms, while acid soils produce the blues. Large, green, shiny leaves appear mid-spring and dome-shaped flower heads appear during summer. ❀ **PLANTING** In cooler regions, hydrangeas will grow quite happily in full sun. In warmer districts, choose a protected and lightly shaded position. The soil should be rich, moist, and well drained, and planting can occur at any time of year. ❀ **FLOWERING** Blooms appear from summer through to autumn. ❀ **CULTIVATION** Keep well watered throughout summer and fertilize during spring. Hydrangeas produce flowers on two-year-old wood, so remove the spent blooms immediately to give the plant a chance to produce new, vigorous growth. ❀ **PROPAGATION** Easily propagated from softwood cuttings taken in late spring or early summer, or semi-hardwood cuttings from mid to late summer.

Kerria japonica 'Pleniflora'
Jew's Mallow ○ ◑ ❖❖❖

✿ **OTHER NAME** Kerria ✿ **DESCRIPTION** A graceful, deciduous shrub with long, arching canes that bear clusters of double, golden yellow blooms from mid-spring. Occasionally, the odd flower will also appear in summer and early autumn. The branches reach 7–10 feet (2–3 m) in height with an equal spread and have an open, angular appearance. Bright green, sharply toothed leaves appear during early spring, and in colder climates they develop rich, autumn tones. Jew's mallow looks best in mixed shrub borders but can be grown as solitary specimens, provided it has some protection from strong sun and winds. ✿ **PLANTING** A hardy plant in most soils, it prefers those that are rich in nutrients and free draining. Choose a protected area with light shade or full sun and plant in spring. Enrich the surrounding soil with compost or leaf mould to get them off to a flying start. ✿ **FLOWERING** From mid-spring for a period of three weeks. ✿ **CULTIVATION** Jew's mallow requires occasional, deep waterings in the growing season. Adding compost and general purpose fertilizer in spring will sustain the vigorous growth. After flowering, non-productive branches should be cut back to ground level, otherwise prune lightly to a compact shape. Trim frost-damaged tips in early spring. ✿ **PROPAGATION** By softwood cuttings in summer, or division in autumn.

Leycesteria formosa
Pheasant berry ○ ❖❖

✿ **OTHER NAME** Partridge berry, Formosa honeysuckle

✿ **DESCRIPTION** A striking, upright, deciduous shrub that is valued for both its foliage and flowers. It is an adaptable plant that prefers an open, sunny position and moderately rich, well-drained soil that has been enriched with organic matter, but not over-fertilized. It grows to 9 feet (3 m) with a pleasant, rounded shape and a good covering of oval, deep green foliage. The funnel-shaped flowers are most attractive, white in colour with very prominent purple-red bracts; they are borne in pendulous clusters. The flowers are followed by dark red-purple fruits. The partridge berry is an ideal feature plant for the back of a mixed border. ✿ **PLANTING** Plant in spring or summer in well-prepared soil, digging a hole that is at least twice the size of the root ball. Water in well, and keep watering regularly, especially in hot weather, until the plant is well established. ✿ **FLOWERING** The flowers appear during summer, followed by the berries in autumn. ✿ **CULTIVATION** Once established this plant is quite low maintenance, although it benefits from an annual mulch of well-rotted organic matter, such as compost.

✿ **PROPAGATION** The plant can be divided in autumn, or propagated by cuttings taken in summer.

Ligustrum ovalifolium
Oval-leaved privet ○ ◑ ❖❖❖

✿ **OTHER NAME** California privet ✿ **DESCRIPTION** Privet is a widely-grown, evergreen shrub prized for its suitability for hedging and ability to withstand both drought and city pollution. When untended, the Oval-leaved privet reaches 15 feet (4.5 m) in height, spreading 10 feet (3 m). The foliage is dense, upright, glossy, and dark green in appearance. A variegated form is also available, known as *Ligustrum ovalifolium* 'Aureum'. During summer, dense panicles of tubular, white flowers appear that, unfortunately, emit a rather unpleasant scent and cause allergies in sensitive people. The flowers are followed by rounded, bluish-black berries in autumn.

✿ **PLANTING** Plant during spring or autumn in full sun or part shade. Virtually any soil type will be tolerated, provided it is well drained. Plantings for formal hedging should be spaced at 1–2 feet (30–60 cm) intervals. Tip prune at planting time if necessary. ✿ **FLOWERING** Flowers appear midsummer, followed by tiny, black fruits. ✿ **CULTIVATION** Feed with well-rotted manure during spring and keep moist throughout summer. Prune hedges twice a year, during early spring and again in late summer, to prevent self-seeding. Remove dead branches from solitary specimens during spring to maintain their natural, graceful appearance. ✿ **PROPAGATION** By seed or semi-ripe cuttings taken in autumn.

Lonicera fragrantissima
Winter honeysuckle ○ ◑ ❖❖❖

❀ **DESCRIPTION** For a splash of winter colour, you cannot go past the winter honeysuckle. An irresistibly-fragrant shrub that grows to a useful height of 6 feet (2 m) and spreads to about 8 feet (2.5 m). Perfect for use in perennial borders, near fences, pathways, and windows, or any position where its sweet scent can be fully appreciated. Winter honeysuckle can be semi-evergreen or deciduous and has gracefully arching branches with tough, leathery, green leaves. During late winter or early spring, creamy-white flowers put on a welcome display. ❀ **PLANTING** Winter honeysuckles are best planted during autumn and will tolerate a wide range of soil types and situations. They prefer a sunny position with well-drained soil and plenty of room to spread. ❀ **FLOWERING** Flowers appear from late winter to early spring and flower throughout the season. ❀ **CULTIVATION** Winter honeysuckles require very little maintenance. Once established, they are quite resistant to drought and frost. In situations where there is sufficient room to grow, no pruning is required except to remove old or damaged branches. This should be carried out during autumn. ❀ **PROPAGATION** Cuttings can be taken at any time of year.

Osteospermum ecklonis
White veldt daisy ○ ❖❖❖

✿ **OTHER NAME** White African daisy ✿ **DESCRIPTION** Hardy, fast growing, and long-flowering are the main characteristics of these striking perennial plants. Osteospermums are perfect for that hot spot in the garden, on steep banks, or for cascading over retaining walls. The speed at which they grow makes them effective weed suppressors, and they are able to thrive despite poor, impoverished soil. *Osteospermum ecklonis* grows to a height of 3 feet (90 cm) with an equal spread. The flowers are pure-white, daisy-shaped and have smart, navy blue centres. The leaves are narrow and oval in shape. ✿ **PLANTING** For best results, plant during spring or summer and choose a sunny position with light, well-drained soil. The warmer the position, the longer the flowering period. Avoid boggy, low-lying areas and plant in clusters of three for an eye-catching display.
✿ **FLOWERING** Flowers appear from late winter through to spring in warmer regions, and from summer to autumn in cooler zones.
✿ **CULTIVATION** Once established, this daisy requires minimal attention. It tolerates drought and only requires occasional watering. Dress with pulverized manure during spring and trim back excess growth during autumn to maintain bushiness. ✿ **PROPAGATION** Take semi-hardwood cuttings inlate summer or sow seed during early spring.

Pseudosasa japonica (syn. *Arundinaria japonica*)
Bamboo ○ pH ❖❖

❖ **OTHER NAME** Arrow bamboo ❖ **DESCRIPTION** Useful for screening, windbreak, or waterside, arrow bamboo is grown for its highly-decorative foliage. It originates from Japan, and not surprisingly, is often featured in Japanese-style gardens throughout the world. It is evergreen and grows to a height of 15 feet (4.5 m), with the capacity to spread endlessly throughout the garden if permitted. The graceful stems are clumping, arching, and dull green in appearance. They produce long, glossy, pointed leaves up to 1 foot (30 cm) in length, with greyish-green undersides. The sheaths are brown and pubescent. ❖ **PLANTING** Plant during spring in a sunny, protected position. The soil should be moist, well drained, and slightly alkaline. Choose an area where spreading roots will be restricted, such as a position between a pathway and wall. Otherwise, some other form of barrier can be inserted deeply into the soil around the plant to prevent indiscriminate spreading. ❖ **FLOWERING** Flowers are inconspicuous.
❖ **CULTIVATION** Minimal maintenance is required, apart from occasional deep waterings throughout the growing season, and the application of well-rotted compost or manure during spring to induce plenty of lush, new growth. Prune only to remove dying or overcrowded canes during autumn.
❖ **PROPAGATION** By division in autumn.

Pyracantha angustifolia

Firethorn ○ ● ❖❖

❀ **DESCRIPTION** A delightful, evergreen shrub that grows to 10 feet (3 m) with a spread of 6 feet (about 2 m). Firethorns make excellent hedging plants near walls or fences, or they can be grown as small trees. If you enjoy birds in the garden be sure to plant one, as the thorny, heavily foliaged limbs offer great protection for our feathered friends. During summer, tiny, white flowers appear. These are promptly followed by masses of bright, orangy-red berries. ❀ **PLANTING** Firethorns can be planted out at any time of year in most positions, and in virtually any type of soil provided they have reasonable drainage. They will tolerate full sun or shade and can withstand polluted and windy conditions. It is wise not to plant them near bushland areas, however, where they can become a menace.

❀ **FLOWERING** Flowers appear throughout summer, followed by clusters of berries during autumn and early winter. ❀ **CULTIVATION** Keep on the dry side during summer, feed during spring, and prune to encourage branching. Pruning can be carried out at any time of year, but it may reduce the number of flowers and berries produced the following season. ❀ **PROPAGATION** Take heeled cuttings during summer, or propagate from stratified seed.

Ribes sanguineum
Flowering currant ○ ◑ ❖❖❖

✿ **OTHER NAME** Pink flowering currant ✿ **DESCRIPTION** The flowering currant is the ornamental cousin of the edible variety and is a favourite in cool climate gardens. During spring, a profusion of heavily scented, pink blooms emerge in decorative, pendulant clusters. A range of new cultivars has also been developed that produce flowers in shades of white, red, and crimson. These are followed in autumn by blue-black, inedible berries. The leaves too are aromatic, deeply incised, and are borne on spiny, arching stems that grow 7–8 feet (2–2.5 m) high, spreading a similar distance. In frosty regions, the leaves develop reddish tints before falling to the ground. ✿ **PLANTING** The flowering currant is tolerant of a variety of soils but thrives best in soil that is moist and well drained. Choose an open position in full sun or part shade and plant anytime between autumn to early spring. Prior to planting, enrich the soil with a good measure of well-rotted compost. ✿ **FLOWERING** Flowers appear during spring, followed by berries in autumn. ✿ **CULTIVATION** Keep moist throughout summer, and mulch to conserve soil moisture. Annual dressings of compost and manure during spring are beneficial. After flowering, prune older stems back to ground level to maintain an open habit. ✿ **PROPAGATION** By hardwood cuttings in winter.

Rosmarinus officinalis

Rosemary ○ ◑ ❖❖❖

✿ **DESCRIPTION** Rosemary is a highly aromatic, evergreen shrub and popular culinary herb that grows to about 3 feet (1 m) high. The flowers are mauve, or blue, and scented, but the small, linear leaves give the plant its wonderfully-pungent reputation. Rosemary is frequently used for cooking. It is also attractive to bees. ✿ **PLANTING** Choose a position near the kitchen door for easy access, or grow near pathways where the scent can be enjoyed. A well-drained, sunny position is preferred, although light shade can be tolerated. Some protection from wind is also desirable. Plant at any time of year. ✿ **FLOWERING** The first flowers appear during spring and carry through until summer. ✿ **CULTIVATION** Rosemary requires very little attention once established. The soil should be kept just moist, as too much water will shorten the length of its life. An application of compost and blood and bone during spring is beneficial. Slow-release fertilizer will also do the trick. Little pruning is required except to remove any straggly growth. Although this is best carried out during autumn, frost-damaged wood may be removed during early spring. ✿ **PROPAGATION** Take heeled cuttings during summer, autumn, or winter from strong side shoots. Bottom heat will speed up the striking process.

Salvia leucantha
Mexican bush sage ○ ❖❖❖

✿ **DESCRIPTION** Mexican bush sage is a favourite for cottage gardens and mild climate areas. It is an attractive evergreen shrub that reaches 2 feet (60 cm) with a spread of 3 feet (1 m), which makes it an ideal plant for perennial borders in warmer areas. In cooler areas use as a summer bedding or greenhouse plant. This plant has delightful, velvety, violet and white flower spikes that contrast well with the whitish leaves. The flowers are long lasting and look most attractive in floral arrangements. ✿ **PLANTING** Plant during spring or autumn in an open, sunny position where the soil is light and well drained. To give the plant a good start, place some friable compost mixed with surrounding soil, into the hole prior to planting. Keep moist during the initial establishment period. ✿ **FLOWERING** Flowers appear through autumn and winter. ✿ **CULTIVATION** Mexican sage tolerates drought once established, so water sparingly throughout the growing season. A light application of complete fertilizer, slow-release pellets, or pulverized manure during spring is ideal. Prune the plant back hard during spring and new growth will soon emerge at ground level. Young plants may require protection from frost in cooler districts.
✿ **PROPAGATION** Mexican sage may be divided and transplanted during autumn, or propagated by cuttings during autumn.

Spiraea cantoniensis
Chinese spiraea ○ ◑ ❖❖❖

❀ **OTHER NAME** Reeves' spiraea ❀ **DESCRIPTION** *Spiraea cantoniensis* is a deciduous shrub, known for its arching stems in reddish tones and its showy clusters of white flowers. The shrub itself is not particularly attractive for a large part of the year, however, the highly ornamental blooms are definitely worth the wait. It can grow to a height of 6 feet (2 m) and spreads widely, making it an ideal plant to cover that unsightly fence or wall. The dark green, diamond-shaped leaves develop reddish tones during autumn. ❀ **PLANTING** Plant in a sunny or partly shaded position during spring or early summer. The soil pH is not important, provided the soil is rich and well drained. Dig in generous quantities of compost and manure prior to planting, and allow sufficient room for spreading. ❀ **FLOWERING** Heavy flower clusters hang gracefully from the ends of the branches during late spring and early summer. ❀ **CULTIVATION** Spiraeas must be kept moist, so mulch well to retain soil moisture. Feed during early spring. The flowers of *Spiraea cantoniensis* appear only on the current season's growth. Prune during early spring before the new growth begins. ❀ **PROPAGATION** Cuttings may be taken at any time of year.

Viburnum opulus
Guelder rose ○ ❖❖❖

❀ **OTHER NAME** European cranberry bush ❀ **DESCRIPTION**
A spectacular shrub when in flower that grows to 12 feet (3.5 m) in height
with a spread of 7 feet (2 m). Guelder rose is deciduous in nature and carries
broad, deeply lobed, green leaves that redden during autumn. It can
withstand frost and pollution. The flowers are deeply perfumed, white, and
form attractive, flattened, spherical clusters during spring. After flowering,
translucent red berries form and remain on the shrub throughout winter.
Birds do not find these attractive. ❀ **PLANTING** Best grown near
pathways in a sunny position protected from cold winds. The soil needs to
be rich and moisture retentive for best results, but the soil's pH is of no real
concern. Plant anytime between autumn and spring into well-prepared soil.
❀ **FLOWERING** Flowers appear from late spring through to early
summer, followed promptly by long-lasting, berries. ❀ **CULTIVATION**
Keep viburnums well watered. Pruning should be limited to the removal of
dead branches in order to maintain the plant's naturally graceful shape. This
is best carried out during spring. Feed during spring to maintain healthy
growth and mulch the surrounding soil if it has a tendency to dry out.
❀ **PROPAGATION** Cuttings strike readily from softwood, semi-
hardwood, or hardwood taken from late spring to winter.

Weigela florida

Weigela ◑ ❖❖❖

❀ **DESCRIPTION** Weigela is a deciduous shrub that can reach a height of 6–8 feet (2–2.5 m). For much of the year these shrubs go unnoticed, but the spring blooms steal the show when revealed. Arching canes produce pale to deep pink blooms and a variety of cultivars exist, including the popular *Weigela florida* 'Variegata', with its creamy-white variegated leaves and baby-pink blooms; 'Bristol Ruby', with its deep red flowers; and 'Candida', which has pure-white flowers. It is a useful border plant and grows best in cool to mild climate areas. ❀ **PLANTING** Plant during spring into rich, well-drained soil. Full sun burns the tender leaves, so choose a lightly shaded position for best results. Weigelas are at home when planted against a fence, or when nestled amongst other shrubs. ❀ **FLOWERING** Weigelas parade their blooms from late spring to early summer. ❀ **CULTIVATION** Water generously, and mulch to conserve soil moisture. Supplement the soil with a complete fertilizer or animal manure during spring. Prune after flowering and remove old canes every few years. Dying tips can be removed during spring. ❀ **PROPAGATION** Cuttings can be taken at any time of year.

Actinidia deliciosa
Kiwi fruit ○ ◑ pH ❖❖❖

✿ **OTHER NAME** Chinese gooseberry ✿ **DESCRIPTION** The kiwi fruit is a deciduous climber, widely grown for its soft, edible fruits. In its natural habitat, it is accustomed to twining its way up tall forest trees but in the garden, it grows happily over fences and vertical supports. The vines are capable of climbing anywhere from 6 to 50 feet (1.8 to 15 m) but are easily kept under control. The large leaves are lime green, rounded and covered in fine hairs. The white flowers are bell-shaped and hang in clusters, while the fruits are oval with emerald-green, fleshy interiors. ✿ **PLANTING** The plants are either male or female, so you will require at least one of each in order to produce fruit. They should be planted during late winter into well-drained, slightly acid, sandy loam and given plenty of room to spread. Kiwi fruit has a high requirement for water so mulching is essential, and strong trellising is required to support the vine. ✿ **FLOWERING** Flowers appear during summer followed by fruits in autumn. ✿ **CULTIVATION** Water frequently, particularly during the crucial fruit-set stage. Apply a high nitrogen fertilizer during early spring and top-dress with animal manure each autumn. Prune during winter and remove unwanted, upright shoots throughout summer. ✿ **PROPAGATION** From seed or cuttings.

Akebia quinata
Chocolate vine ○ ❖❖❖

✿ **OTHER NAME** Five-leaf akebia ✿ **DESCRIPTION** A useful woody-stemmed, twining climber that tends to be evergreen in climates that experience mild winters, and deciduous in cool to cold climates. Chocolate vine is a moderately vigorous plant with attractive mid-green foliage and subtle brownish-purple flowers that have a delightful vanilla fragrance, followed by interesting fruits. In the right conditions, this climber can grow to 30 feet (10 m) or more, however it is quite easy to keep under control with routine pruning. It can withstand winter frosts. ✿ **PLANTING** Chocolate vine will grow well in open, sunny position in moderately rich and well-drained soil, against a fence or trellis that will provide adequate support. Add some well-rotted organic matter to the soil prior to planting. ✿ **FLOWERING** The flowers appear in late spring to early summer. ✿ **CULTIVATION** Water well in summer, and mulch around the base of plants to suppress weeds. They do not appreciate disturbances, so avoid cultivating around the base of plants, or attempting to transplant established vines. A slow-release fertilizer, applied in spring, will keep the plant growing steadily all year long. ✿ **PROPAGATION** The vine is easy to propagate by layering in winter or taking semi-ripe cuttings in summer.

Campsis radicans

Trumpet creeper ○ ❖❖❖

✿ **OTHER NAME** Trumpet vine ✿ **DESCRIPTION** A vigorous woody-stemmed climber that can reach 20 feet (7 m) if not trimmed, with masses of toothed leaves that have a downy undersurface. The flower display of this vine is quite dramatic, with many pendulous clusters of showy, trumpet-shaped flowers that are in the red, orange, and yellow colour range. This is an excellent vine for temperate climates, and although it can withstand frost, it will probably require a sunny wall if grown in cooler climates. It will require the support of a fence, trellis, or pergola to display it effectively. ✿ **PLANTING** One plant will cover a large area, and should be planted into well-prepared, fertile soil that has had plenty of organic matter added in the form of well-rotted compost. Good drainage is essential. ✿ **FLOWERING** Late summer and autumn are the main flowering periods. ✿ **CULTIVATION** Water well until established, but take care not to overwater if drainage is not excellent. During hot summer weather, make sure the soil retains some moisture; prune lightly in spring to encourage good flowering. ✿ **PROPAGATION** Take semi-ripe cuttings in summer, or layer the lower stems in winter.

Clematis montana

Anemone clematis ○ ◑ pH ❖❖❖

❀ **OTHER NAME** Clemantis ❀ **DESCRIPTION** The anemone
clematis is a beautiful, deciduous climber that spreads rapidly over walls,
fences, pergolas, and tall trees, reaching an eventual height of up to 25 feet
(7.5 m) if left unpruned. The flowers are profuse, scented and are white or
pastel pink according to the variety. They are soon followed by decorative
clusters of feathery seeds which hang on throughout winter, and self-seed
readily the following spring. The leaves are mid to purplish-green, are
arranged in groups of three, and have toothed margins. ❀ **PLANTING**
Plant in a sunny position during spring. It is important to provide a cool
root run by mulching and strategically placing large stones or small shrubs
in front of this climber. The soil should be moist, light, and well drained,
although heavier soils can be tolerated. A slightly alkaline to neutral pH is
best. Prior to planting, erect a sturdy trellis or lattice frame as a form of
support. ❀ **FLOWERING** During late spring. ❀ **CULTIVATION** It is
important to water regularly throughout spring and summer. Feed during
spring with a complete fertilizer and prune after flowering. Remove the
spent flowers if you do not wish them to self-seed throughout the garden,
and be sure never to cultivate around the shallow roots.
❀ **PROPAGATION** By seed or division.

Petunia hybrids
Common garden petunia ○ pH

❀ **DESCRIPTION** For a dazzling annual display, you cannot go past the petunia. Its large, cheery blooms are available in an amazing variety of colours, including pink, white, red, purple, yellow, blue, and salmon shades. Two-tone combinations are also very popular. Dwarf types reach 6–8 inches (15–20 cm), while taller varieties may grow as high as 1 foot (30 cm). Many are scented, although some of the new varieties have lost this attribute.

❀ **PLANTING** Plant seedlings during early spring into a sunny position with moist, loamy, well-drained soil. Poorer soils may be built up with compost prior to planting, and a little lime should be added if the soil is on the acid side. Space seedlings 8 inches (20 cm) apart.

❀ **FLOWERING** From summer through to autumn. ❀ **CULTIVATION** Petunias need to be watered regularly throughout the growing season, but go easy on the nitrogenous fertilizer to prevent excessive foliage growth at the expense of the flowers. Phosphorous-based fertilizers will often give better results. Faded blooms should be pinched off regularly with your fingertips to extend the flowering period. Lightly trim the plants during late summer to induce an autumn flush. Virus-infected petunias should be removed immediately. ❀ **PROPAGATION** By seed sown under glass during early spring.

Scabiosa atropurpurea
Sweet scabious ○ pH

✿ **OTHER NAME** Pincushion flower, Mournful widow
✿ **DESCRIPTION** An upright, bushy plant growing to 3 feet (1 m) in height, spreading to 1 foot (30 cm). Scabiosa is an attractive plant with a good covering of mid-green, lance-shaped leaves and domed pincushion flowers that are deep crimson in colour and pleasantly fragrant. The flowers are borne on tall, wiry stems, making a pretty display. There are now also taller-growing and dwarf forms available, with flowers that include white, pink, purple, and blue. Scabiosa is a charming plant for a cottage bed or border. ✿ **PLANTING** Plant seeds or seedlings in fertile, well-drained soil in autumn for a spring display, or in early spring for summer flowering. If growing from seed, keep the ground lightly moist until germination is successful. ✿ **FLOWERING** Spring or summer, depending on when the seeds or seedlings are planted. ✿ **CULTIVATION** Mulch around the young plants when established, taking care not to take the mulch layer too close to the stems of the plants. Water well, especially in hot weather, and use a liquid fertilizer during the growth period to encourage flowering. The flowers are excellent for cutting and arranging. ✿ **PROPAGATION** By seed, which can be collected from the dried flower heads in autumn.

Tropaeolum majus
Garden nasturtium ○ ◐

✿ **OTHER NAME** Common nasturtium ✿ **DESCRIPTION** The common nasturtium is a fast-growing annual and is a welcome addition in any garden. New varieties are compact in shape, reaching 10 inches (25 cm) in height with a spread of 10–18 inches (25–45 cm). Climbing forms may reach 8 feet (2.5 m) in height. The fragrant flowers are brightly coloured in shades of yellow, orange, and red, and the rounded leaves make a crispy addition to salads. Compact nasturtium varieties grow best along borders or as fillers in garden beds. Climbing varieties will take advantage of nearby trees for support or will happily cascade over walls and banks.

✿ **PLANTING** Nasturtiums grow easily from seed sown during early spring. The soil should preferably be sandy or well drained, as fertile soil will produce lush growth at the expense of the flowers. Choose a sunny position for best results, and sow the seed at 1 foot (30 cm) intervals.

✿ **FLOWERING** From summer to autumn. ✿ **CULTIVATION** Keep nasturtiums on the dry side. New growth can be trimmed at any time if it threatens to take over, and the seeds of your favourite varieties can be easily collected after flowering. Aphids and caterpillars are the main pests of the common nasturtium. ✿ **PROPAGATION** By seed in spring.

INDEX OF BOTANICAL NAMES

INDEX OF COMMON NAMES

PHOTOGRAPHY CREDITS

The Garden Picture Library: front cover and p.61(Linda Burgess), p.11 (Roger Hyam), p.12 Bob Challinor), p.13 (David Russell), p.15 (Brian Carter), p.17 (Didier Willery), p.19 (Brian Carter), p.20 (David Russell), p.27 (Brian Carter), p.28 (JS Sira), p.31 (John Glover), p.40 (David Russell), p.43 (Brian Carter), p.45 (John Glover), p.46 (Brigitte Thomas), p.47 (Paul Windsor), p.51(Brian Carter), p.52 (Clive Boursnell), p.55 (David Russell), p.64 (Jerry Pavia), p.74 (Morley Read), p.76 (John Glover), p.81 (Paul Windsor), p.83 (John Glover), p.85 (Didier Willery), p.87 (John Glover), p.90 (Jerry Pavia), p.108 (Brian Carter); **Ivy Hansen Photography:** p.10, p.14, p.16, p.21, p.22, p.23, p.24, p.26, p.29, p.30, p.33,p.34, p.35, p. 36, p.37, p.38, p.39, p.41, p.4 2, p.44, p.48, p.49, p.50, p.53, p.54, p.56, p.57, p.58, p.59, p.60, p.62, p.63, p.65, p.66, p.69, p.70, p.71, p.72, p.73, p.75, p.77, p.79, p.80, p.84, p.88, p.91, p.92, p.93, p.95, p.96, p.97, p.98, p.99, p.100, p.101, p.102, p.103, p.105, p.106, p.107, p.109; **Horizon Photo Library:** p.82; **S&O Mathews:** p.32, p.61, p.68, p.78, p.86, p.89, p.94; **Lorna Rose:** p.18, p.25, p.67, p.104